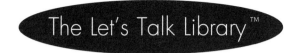

The Let's Talk Library™

# Let's Talk About Deafness

Melanie Apel Gordon

The Rosen Publishing Group's

PowerKids Press™
New York

For Ethan and Hayley (and Hayley's "stuffy" ears) in Ireland. Love, Melanie.

Published in 1999 by The Rosen Publishing Group, Inc.
29 East 21st Street, New York, NY 10010

First Edition

Book Design: Erin McKenna

Photo Credits: Cover, pp. 4, 11, 12, 15, 16, 20, by Seth Dinnerman; p. 7 © Michael Goodman/ FPG International; p. 19 © Barbarra Peacock.

Gordon, Melanie Apel.
    Let's talk about deafness / by Melanie Apel Gordon.
        p.      cm. — (The Let's talk library)
    Includes index.
    Summary: Discusses deafness, its causes, and how deaf people cope with their condition and live full lives despite their inability to hear.
    ISBN 0-8239-5198-7
    1.Deafness—Juvenile literature.  2. Deaf—Juvenile literature. [1. Deaf.  2. Physically handicapped.]
I. Title. II. Series.
RF291.37.G67 1998
617.8—dc21                                                             97-48363
                                                                            CIP
                                                                            AC

Manufactured in the United States of America

# Table of Contents

| 1 | Eva's Noisy House | 5 |
| 2 | Why Are Some People Deaf? | 6 |
| 3 | How Ears Work | 9 |
| 4 | Why Can't Some People Hear? | 10 |
| 5 | Sign Language | 13 |
| 6 | Lipreading | 14 |
| 7 | Deaf People Can Talk | 17 |
| 8 | Hearing Aids | 18 |
| 9 | Making Life Easier | 21 |
| 10 | Be Anything You Want to Be | 22 |
| | Glossary | 23 |
| | Index | 24 |

# Eva's Noisy House

It's a busy afternoon at Eva's house. Max is watching cartoons on TV. Billy is practicing his trumpet. The dog is barking at the doorbell. The phone is ringing, and Tess shouts, "I'll get it!" Max yells at the dog, and Tess yells at Max to be quiet. Eva is sitting on the sofa reading a book. The noise in her house does not bother her at all because she can't hear it. Eva is **deaf** (DEF). When a person is deaf, it means he or she cannot hear.

◀ Deaf people cannot hear the noises around them.

# Why Are Some People Deaf?

People are deaf for different reasons. Some people are born deaf. They may have deaf parents or deaf **siblings** (SIH-blingz). Other people lose their hearing because of an illness. Some illnesses can hurt part of the ear so that a person can't hear. People who work around very loud noises for a long time may also become deaf. Or people who get hit very hard on the head may lose their hearing. About 2 million people in the United States are deaf.

Construction workers who are around loud machines all day may lose their hearing. ▶

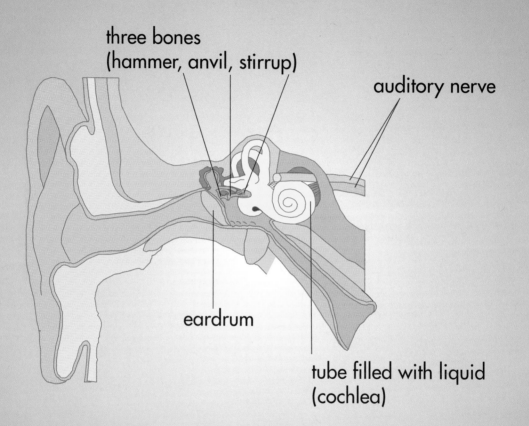

three bones
(hammer, anvil, stirrup)

auditory nerve

eardrum

tube filled with liquid
(cochlea)

# How Ears Work

Inside your ear is an **eardrum** (EER-drum). Sound goes into your ear as a **vibration** (vy-BRAY-shun) and moves the eardrum. Next, three tiny bones vibrate in the middle part of the ear. Then sound moves to the inner ear where there are tubes with liquid in them. The vibrations make the liquid move and this sends special signals to your brain through the **auditory nerve** (AW-dih-tor-ee NERV). Finally your brain tells you that you hear a sound! It takes less than one second for all of this to happen.

◀ This is a drawing of what the inside of your ear looks like.

# Why Can't Some People Hear?

Some people can't hear because part of their ear isn't working right. Maybe the eardrum has been torn. When the eardrum heals after it is torn, scars form and make it less **flexible** (FLEK-sih-bul). Then the eardrum can't vibrate as well. Sometimes the bones in the ears don't move right. If this happens, then you can't hear. If **cells** (SELZ) inside the ear get hurt, they can't move vibrations along. And then you can't hear. Sometimes you can't hear because part of your brain is not working right.

Your doctor can look at your eardrum and tell you if it's healthy or not. ▶

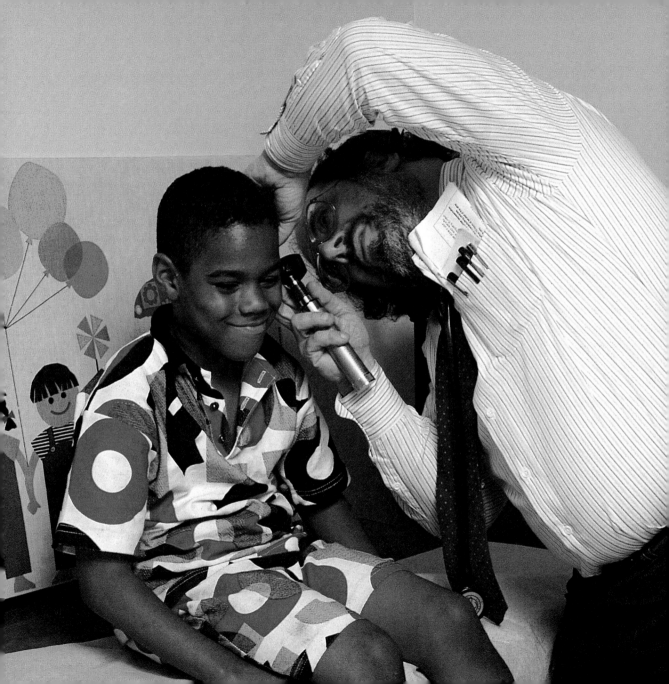

# Sign Language

We all like to talk to each other. But because deaf people can't hear, they **communicate** (kuh-MYOO-nih-kayt) in different ways. Some deaf people use **sign language** (SYN LANG-gwij) to talk to each other. Sign language is a way of using your body instead of your voice to "speak." You move your hands, fingers, and face to make different shapes. The shapes are the signs for letters, words, numbers, names, and ideas. People who can hear often learn sign language so they can communicate with deaf friends or family members.

◀ Sign language is good to know, whether or not you or a family member is deaf.

# Lipreading

Deaf people often want to communicate with people who do not know sign language. So many deaf people learn to read lips. They watch a person's mouth as he or she is talking. Then they can tell what words the person is saying by the shapes that his or her lips make. It takes time to learn how to read lips. But when a deaf person can read lips, then she can join any **conversation** (kon-ver-SAY-shun).

You can better understand what someone is saying by watching their lips move. You ▶ don't have to be deaf to read lips!

# Deaf People Can Talk

It's hard to learn how to talk if you can't hear the sounds that you want to make. But many deaf people do learn to talk. With their hands, they can feel the vibrations that words make in another person's throat. Then they can practice making the same vibrations in their own throats. They learn to use their lips and tongue to say words. They also learn how to make their voices loud or soft.

If you place your hands on your friend's throat as he speaks, you can feel the vibrations that his words make!

# Hearing Aids

A hearing aid is a small piece of plastic that fits inside your ear. It makes sounds louder, but it does not make sounds clearer. Some deaf people wear hearing aids to help them hear some sounds. For some people, hearing aids help them hear much better. For other people, hearing aids help only a little bit.

This boy wears a hearing aid so he can hear his classmates better. ▶

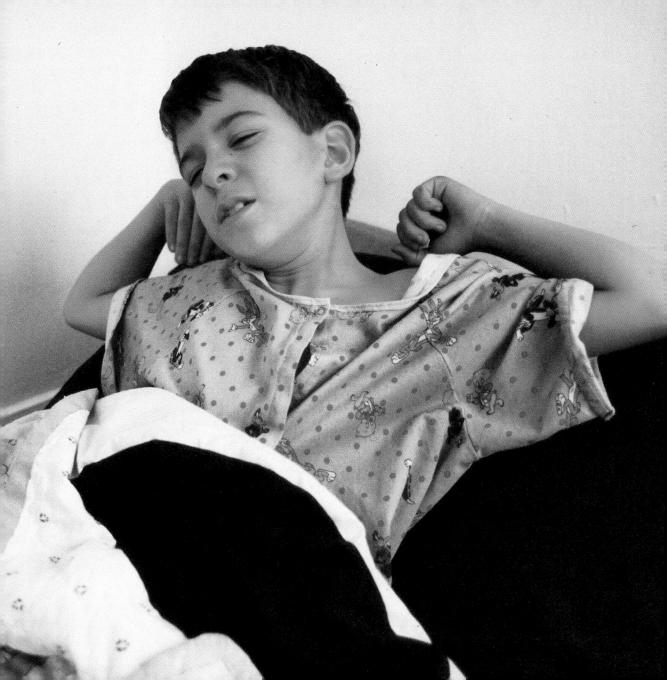

# Making Life Easier

Lots of things can make your life easier if you are deaf. People who can hear wake up in the morning to the buzzing of an alarm clock. The alarm on a deaf person's clock may be a vibrating bed or a bright, flashing light instead of a buzzer. Lights in your house can also let you know when someone is ringing your doorbell, or when the baby is crying. A special service can help you use the telephone. With this service, you type your message to a friend. Then an operator types your friend's message back to you.

◀ A vibrating bed or a flashing light can wake up a person who is deaf.

# Be Anything You Want to Be

Kids who are deaf can do the same things that their hearing friends do. Deaf kids go to school, play sports, read books, and dance. Even though they can't hear music, deaf people can feel the vibrations and the rhythm of the music. Marlee Matlin is a famous deaf actress. She has been in plays, in movies, and on TV. Ludwig van Beethoven, a famous composer, wrote one of his most famous works after he became deaf. Deaf kids can grow up to be anything they want to be.

22

# Glossary

**auditory nerve** (AW-dih-tor-ee NERV)  The nerve that carries signals from the middle ear to the brain.

**cell** (SEL)  The basic building block of all living things.

**communicate** (kuh-MYOO-nih-kayt)  To share information or feelings.

**conversation** (kon-ver-SAY-shun)  When people talk to each other.

**deaf** (DEF)  When a person can't hear.

**eardrum** (EER-drum)  A thin sheet of skin inside the ear.

**flexible** (FLEK-sih-bul)  Being able to move and bend in many ways.

**siblings** (SIH-blingz)  Your brothers and sisters.

**sign language** (SYN LANG-gwij)  Using your face and body to communicate with others.

**vibration** (vy-BRAY-shun)  Fast back-and-forth movements that you can feel.

# Index

**A**
auditory nerve, 9

**B**
Beethoven, Ludwig
     van, 22
brain, 9, 10

**C**
cells, 10
communication,
     13, 14, 17
conversation, 14

**E**
eardrum, 9, 10

**H**
hearing aid, 18

**I**
inner ear, 9

**L**
lipreading, 14

**M**
Matlin, Marlee, 22

**R**
reasons for
     deafness, 6,
     10

**S**
siblings, 6
sign language,
     13, 14

**T**
talking, 17
telephone, 21

**V**
vibrations, 9, 10,
     17, 21, 22